What If?

LONI HUNLEY

What If?

ISBN (Paperback): 979-8-89672-112-3
ISBN (Hardback): 979-8-89672-114-7
ISBN (Ebook): 979-8-89672-113-0

PROMINENT
BOOKS

5830 E 2nd St, Ste 7000 #9983
Casper, WY 82609
USA

Introduction

"What if?"

Those are the two words I heard in 2019, sitting in my office. I knew then God was telling me this would be the title of a book I would write. Two simple words, and yet what they ask can have tremendous meaning.

First, let me introduce myself. My name is Loni. I am a daughter, sister, wife, mother, and "Nana" to my super cute and special grandchildren, Jolie and Seely! I am a court reporter for Victorville Superior Court, a career that has served me well. Most importantly, I am a believer in Jesus Christ, with whom I have the privilege of knowing personally and spending time with and who often directs me to do things outside my comfort zone, like writing a book.

I must say that I have always wanted to be an author. Since I was a little girl, I have loved reading books and being taken away to another time and place, imagining myself as the main character as the story comes to life. But every time I sit down to write a book, the words never end up on the page as they sound in my head. I have written a few Bible studies over the past years, but those are different and seem to flow easier. I do them because they help me study the Word of God in an in-depth way. But this "What if?" I felt the Lord washing this phrase over me. *What if? What if?*

As I have thought about these two little words over the past few years, many different scenarios can apply to them, but for me, it always comes back to the Bible. What if we lived our lives governed by the Word of God? What if, as 2 Timothy 3:16–17 (NKJV) tells us:

> All Scripture is given by inspiration of God, and is profitable for doctrine, for reproof, for correction, for instruction in righteousness, that the man of God may be complete, thoroughly equipped for every good work?

What if we followed it, lived according to the directives contained here, and did not walk in our human desires and will? And what if, by doing that, our lives were remarkably and eternally changed? These two verses are my life verses. I believe them with all my being, and we must start here with this knowledge or what good is our faith? If we as believers don't trust the very Word He has given us as truth, then I have to ask, where is your faith, and on what is it based? God's Word, and our trust and confidence in it as truth and as His inspired Word to us, is foundational to our walk and life in Him.

Lord, I ask You to be the author of my life and this book. May these words written here point others to You and give us all a little food for thought. Amen.

Chapter 1

As I started to think about this book and the possibilities for the content, I believe God firmly told me to begin with the Creation. So let's look at how our Lord created our heavens and earth, and I will ask you to set aside any doubt you have and just accept it for what it says; then we will look at our first "What if" concept.

Grab a Bible, or look one up online or on a Bible app, and turn to Genesis—the very first book in the Bible—and read chapters 1 through 3. Go ahead. I will be here when you are finished.

All done? There you have it, our Creation story, how our world, as we know it, was formed. Isn't that incredible? Our world was created in six days. As I read through these verses, I try to imagine I am there watching it unfold as He brings an amazing masterpiece to life.

Day and night are formed on day 1. There was nothing but darkness, and then suddenly *light*. What an incredible sight!

On day 2, God creates a visible arch of the sky, dividing the waters above and below, and what we know as heaven is called into existence. Imagine for a moment, waters all around, and then a solid formation begins, growing and separating the waters as land appears.

On day 3, the earth and seas, all plant life, and fruit trees begin to rise out of the newly birthed ground. Can you picture the tiny plants pushing up, bringing forth an array of colors and textures?

Next, we see the sun, moon, and stars, bringing division of light and darkness, creating days, seasons, and years, the fourth day. Think about that first sunrise and sunset, the moon and stars twinkling over the night sky—what beauty!

Now picture this, day 5, seeing the oceans filling up with sea life and every winged bird flying back and forth. Magnificent!

Finally, day 6, animals and land creatures of every kind from cattle to insects begin populating the earth. Can you see them walking, running, and drinking water from pools and eating the fresh grass? Then the most remarkable of all, the first man, Adam, is created by God's hand and in His image! What must Adam have felt with that first breath? I believe it was with great wonder and adoration that he gazed upon all the Lord had made.

Our first look at "what if " is: What if God had not created any of this? We would not exist, and neither would our earth or anything above or below it.

As we continue our journey through Genesis, chapters 2 and 3 give a more in-depth look at our beginning. We see God rested on the seventh day, pleased with what He had done. We learn how Adam is formed from the dust and how God Himself breathed life into his nostrils. Adam then is given the privilege of naming every living creature, but no suitable mate is found for him. So we watch as the Lord takes a rib from Adam and makes a woman, bone of his bone, flesh of his flesh, the perfect mate!

But then the story takes a turn. This beautiful garden is called Eden, where Adam and Eve live. The Lord gives them full reign over the garden and the animals there. He gives them a command, and that was to not eat from the tree of knowledge of good and evil.

Unfortunately, we see a tempter come in the shape of a serpent, who entices the couple to eat from this tree, the one that God instructed them to stay away from, and we watch as sin releases into this beautiful world God made. We learn that because of this choice, Adam and Eve can no longer be in the Lord's personal presence because He is Holy and has never sinned, and they are now unclean and unworthy because they disobeyed their Creator by doing the one thing He instructed them not to; thus a great chasm developed—a bridge that humans cannot cross.

Here we find another "What if " scenario: What if Eve had not listened to the serpent? What would our lives be like today? Could we have stayed living in Eden our entire lives? Would no sin have entered our world? Would we be able to walk and converse with the Lord in His very presence, face to face?

I pose these as questions because I believe sin, as a serpent, was already in this world, who was Satan himself in disguise. And we, humans, were lovingly created with freedom to choose. You see, God knew how this whole story was going to unfold, even before He spoke those first words in Genesis 1, "Let there be light." Satan had already made the decision and left God's presence, taking other angels with him, because he wanted to be like God. God then created the earth and has allowed Satan to live here, knowing he would be a great tempter to the humans who reside here and would often lead astray His children.

God knew what Adam, Eve, and all humankind would do before He even created us. It was no surprise for Him. And the great thing about that is He also designed a way to overcome Satan, sin, and all the ugliness that comes with it. His name is Jesus, and we will look at His story later.

So that leads us to bigger "What if " questions:

1. What if God had not created us?
2. What if He had created Adam and Eve simply to be robots, in a sense?
3. What if He had not given them free will to choose?
4. What if He had not allowed Satan to be here?

These are big questions, and for me, the answer is simple: God wants us to come to Him on our own, not forced, not demanded, not commanded, not because we have to. He wants a relationship with us! And He wants it to be a two-way relationship, not one-sided. He wants us to choose Him! What kind of relationship can you have with a robot? We have all seen robots on TV. They are mechanical, do as they are programmed to do, and have no soul, no heart, and no mind of their own. How are we created? In His image. We have a heart, mind, and soul, and we can choose what we do, where we go, and what we believe. He created us to love and seek companionship. God created us to be thinking beings with a choice to make: follow

Him or follow self and the world view, thus following Satan. He wants us to choose Him!

I love that about Him. It shows that He created us in His image. It shows how He is different from the box we all try to put Him in. It shows that He loves us and wants that relationship with us and why He created us in the first place.

Chapter 2

Next, let's look at some of the directives from God and see how they might impact our lives here if everyone followed them. What if we set aside our preconceived notions and thoughts of who He is and just look at what His Word says and how it might affect our interactions with one another?

It's time to grab that Bible again or open your online edition and read Exodus 20. I use both because online, I can easily look up Hebrew, Aramaic, or Greek translations of words while reading through the Strong's Concordance. But there really is nothing else like holding the Word of God in your hands personally! Go ahead and read this chapter, and then come join me back here.

The Ten Commandments, found in Exodus 20:1–17 (Old Testament), state the following:

1. You should have no other gods before Me.
2. Do not make for yourself a carved image.
3. Do not take the name of the Lord your God in vain.
4. Remember the Sabbath.
5. Honor your father and your mother.
6. Do not murder.
7. Do not commit adultery.
8. Do not steal.
9. Do not bear false witness against your neighbor.
10. Do not covet anything of your neighbor.

It is important to note that at the time of the writing of these commandments, a man named Moses and the Israelites were traveling through the desert after escaping Egypt and slavery. That is a whole wonderful, historical story that is well worth reading, so I hope you make time to do that in the near future!

This is a different culture and time, and the commandments were given to these people, God's chosen, who are being led by the Lord on a forty-year trek to a promised land but keep getting delayed in their arrival because of their sin and rebelliousness. That said, these definitely still apply to us today, even in these modern times, and they could greatly help us live much simpler, easier lives if we abided by them.

First one, "You should have no other gods before Me." This is a big one. Again, for the sake of this reading, just accept that He is the only God. Let's think back to the beginning of Genesis and remember who created all this world and the life in it. No other god existed at that time. Other gods came from human imagination. They did not create anything. They are not protecting us or looking out for us. Some have been real people who claimed to be a god, which again is not the truth. The creation of these other gods has done nothing but cause division and difficulties and led people astray. Many of them are carved images, which is the second commandment we will look at.

So what if all humanity had followed the first commandment? Division in faith and race would not exist. I believe this would solve so many of our issues as humans, because we would only have to do what we were created for, to love.

Second, "Do not make for yourself a carved image." This is one that I find very easy to follow, as I have never really understood worshipping something that was made by human hands and called a god. For me, common sense tells us a carved image cannot do anything for us. It is inanimate, has no life, and cannot communicate with us in any way.

Exodus 20:4–6 (NKJV) gives us very detailed instructions:

You shall not make for yourself a carved image—any likeness of anything that is in heaven above, or that is in the earth beneath, or that is in the water under the earth; you shall not bow down to them nor serve them. For I, the Lord your God, am a jealous God, visiting the iniquity of the fathers upon the children to the third and fourth generations of those who hate Me, but showing mercy to thousands, to those who love Me and keep My commandments.

There really is no room for question here what and why the Lord gives this instruction. One, He is a jealous God. Two, it is a sin. He desires to show us mercy and asks only that we keep His commandments, which, when we really look at them, are only to our benefit to follow.

Third, "Do not take the name of the Lord your God in vain." What does that mean? I looked up the word "vain" in Hebrew, and it means in the sense of desolating, evil, emptiness, vanity, falsehood, emptiness of speech, lying, worthlessness. Essentially, don't use any variation of God's name in a bad or negative way. Don't swear by it or use it as profanity. Why? It is disrespectful to our Creator. And He tells us in verse 7 if we do, "the Lord will not hold him guiltless."

Fourth, "Remember the Sabbath." I love this. What if we did "remember the Sabbath"? What if we all took a day of rest one day a week? Say 6:00 p.m. to 6:00 p.m., we have some quiet time (no electronics or TV); hang out with our families; read; visit; play games; take a hike; go sit on an ocean beach, listening to the waves; or spend time as a family, singing some great worship songs and reading and discussing the Word. What might that do for our health or mental health, for our entire bodies?

Verses 9–11 tell us to labor six days and do all our work, but the seventh day is Sabbath, which in Hebrew is *sabat*—intermission, rest. Rest brings rejuvenation. It is also following the example of our Creator who, in six days, created the heavens, earth, and all life, but He rested on the seventh—Sabbath day, blessing it and sanctifying it!

Fifth, "Honor your father and your mother." Verse 12 tells us that by doing this, our "days will be long upon the land which the Lord your God is giving you." Honor is the Hebrew word *kabad* or *kabed*—being used here in a good sense, meaning honorable, treat them with respect. (There is a negative sense too, but not the meaning here.) I know this one can be difficult, especially for those whose parents may not have treated them well. That is another subject in itself, but blessings come for those who can do this. Maybe just forgiving the wrong done by your parent(s) is all the respect you can give, but I believe God honors that!

Sixth, "Do not murder." What if there was no murder? Our jails and courtrooms could be phased out. Families would not be mourning loved ones stolen from them too soon. We could walk down the street unafraid and never hear gunshots in our neighborhood again. Our children could play outside without fear of being accidentally shot by cross fire or kidnapped. Gangs would cease to exist. Hate would lessen and eventually disappear. Peace and love could reign instead of chaos.

Seventh, "Do not commit adultery." This leads me to so many "What if" questions: What if we consulted God about who to marry before taking that huge step or possibly heeded His warning against a prospective partner? What if husbands and wives truly meant the vows they speak at their weddings and are committed to them? What if they stopped thoughts of lust immediately and instead turned their feelings to seeking God and how to love and support their spouse better? Homes would remain intact. Children would have both their parents raising them together, supporting them, guiding them as they grow up. They would have an example of how to be dedicated adults and follow through with commitments.

Eighth, "Do not steal." What if no one took things that did not belong to them? We could leave our doors unlocked. Our children's bikes and toys would not have to be placed in a locked garage when they are not playing with them. Automobiles would remain parked, to be used again by their owners. Employers could rest easy, knowing their money and goods are safe from embezzlement.

Ninth, "Do not bear false witness against your neighbor." Essentially, don't lie and say something false to get another person in trouble. What if we just mind our own business, seek to be kind and even-handed with everyone, even help each other out, instead of trying to see what we can get by hurting one another or taking from one another? Wouldn't life be more peaceful and less stressful?

Tenth, "Do not covet anything of your neighbor." Covet in Hebrew is *hamad* and means to delight in, take pleasure in, desire or lust for. Basically, be happy with what you have. Don't compare what you have to others or think they have something better than you and crave that. This leaves us a very unhappy people, never satisfied, always restless. Be content.

Now we will segue into another commandment from God found in the Old Testament in Deuteronomy 6:5, where we are commanded to love the Lord, our God, with all our heart, soul, and strength. We find this verse again in the New Testament Gospels. One account is in Matthew 22:37–40, where Jesus reiterates Deuteronomy 6:5 and tells us we are to love the Lord with all our heart, soul, strength, and mind. He adds a second onto this that we are to love our neighbor as we love ourselves.

Let's pause here a few minutes, and you go read Deuteronomy 6:5 (Old Testament) and Matthew 22:37–40 (New Testament) for yourself; then come back here, and I will be waiting with another "What if " question.

Welcome back!

What if we could set aside our selfish ways of always seeking what is best for us and instead put others first? Can you imagine what life would be like if we practiced love over hatred? I believe if we strived to follow this guideline, all the rest would fall into place as a natural consequence.

This is a good time to look at some New Testament verses that give us great guidance in how to live. These are the words of Jesus, whom we will look at with more depth in later chapters. So get out your Bible again, and go read Matthew 5; then head back here.

Well? What did you think? So many verses that begin with "Blessed are", and these are perfect "What if" verses to live by. Let's break them down together!

First, we must look at the word "Blessed" and see what the translation in Greek is. It is the word *Makarios*, meaning supremely blest, fortunate, well-off, blessed, happy. Each verse, 3–11, begins with this word and then is followed by who is blessed and how:

Verse 3:

The poor in spirit—meaning the humble.

Theirs is the kingdom of heaven—in their relationship with God, they rise above their circumstances here on earth and are steadfast in faith.

Verse 4:

Those who mourn—grieve.

They shall be comforted—Greek word *Parakaleo*, meaning to call near, beseech, call for.

When my mother passed away, even in mourning for her, I was comforted in knowing she was not struggling to breathe. She was resting in the arms of her Savior.

Verse 5:

The meek—mild, mildness of disposition, gentleness of spirit.

They shall inherit the earth—they are the light shining in this world, able to calmly reply in the face of adversity, submit to God, and set an example.

Verse 6:

Those who hunger and thirst for righteousness—equity, justification.

They shall be filled—satisfied.

Verse 7:

The merciful—compassionate.

They shall obtain mercy—have compassion for others.

Verse 8:

The pure in heart—have right motives, live ethically.

They shall see God—their faith allows them to know God intimately.

Verse 9:

The peacemakers—loving peace.

They shall be called sons of God—they are His children.

Verse 10:

Those who are persecuted for righteousness' sake—these tell others about the Lord, even in the face of adversity or being told not to.

Theirs is the kingdom of heaven—they know whom they serve and their lives are entrusted to Him alone.

Verses 11–12:

The persecuted for their faith—persecuted means made to run or flee, drive away.

Great is your reward in heaven—this speaks of the rewards that God bestows or will bestow for those persecuted for their faith.

What if we lived according to these verses: humbly, grieving evil, in gentleness, equality, mercifully, purely, in peace, not condemning others, sacrificially? Can you even imagine what our lives and those around us would look like? It is nearly impossible, as we have never known a world like this. I do believe though, if we each strive to live our own lives by this, we will see change around us. We can influence others by our grace and peace. Proverbs 15:1 (NKJV) tells us,

> A soft answer often turns away wrath. But a
> harsh word stirs up anger.

That is food for thought as we conclude this chapter! Please take the time to go read the book of Proverbs. It is full of wisdom for life, thirty-one chapters of such goodness! We will not dive into it here, but as you read through, ask yourself "What if" questions. Take your time. Read over again anything that stands out to you, and take notes. If something speaks to you about yourself, think about how you can apply it in your life or make a needed change.

Chapter 3

I feel the Lord is urging a look at Psalm 139, one of my favorites from the book of Psalms. Are you ready to hear a wonderful account of your creation? I hope so! Time to read again. Open that Bible to Psalm 139; read it through. Then read it again, slowly, letting the words settle on you; then come back here, and we will go through it together.

All done? What do you think? What if you take this Psalm and memorize it and whenever you are feeling sad, mad, alone, or any other negative feelings, you remember these beautiful words? It changes our outlook to know that we are loved so much and to this depth!

Verse 1 tells us that the LORD—all caps. *Hmm*, that's interesting. Why is it all caps here? Well, there is only one way to find out. Let's look it up. In Hebrew this particular use of LORD is *yhwh*, which means self-existent or eternal, the proper name of the one true God!

So let's see what the LORD has to say to us here in this Psalm:

1. He searches and knows us.
2. He knows our sitting down and rising up and understands our thoughts afar off.
3. He comprehends our path, our lying down, and is acquainted with all our ways.
4. He knows every word on our tongue! (Ouch! That one is a little sticky at times, isn't it?)

5. He has us completely surrounded—hedged in behind, before, and His hand is upon us.

7–12. These verses give us more context and talk about the Spirit and how we cannot flee from His presence. His hand leads us, holds us, and He shines His light upon us.

13. He has formed our entire bodies and covered us in our mother's womb.

14. He made us fearfully (reverently) and wonderfully.

15. Our frames (body/bones) are not hidden from Him. He took time and carefully created each of us (skillfully wrought).

16. He saw us when we had not yet physically been formed and knew "the days fashioned for us when as yet there were none of them." (Wow!)

The Psalm ends with the author—a man named David—crying out to the *Lord* with gratitude and allegiance and asking Him to lead him (David) in the "the way everlasting," in His presence always.

One thing I want to point out here is there are many of the words in this Psalm that we can look up in the original language to give us more clarity on the meaning, but for our time together, I think we all get the idea—we are lovingly created beings, formed with the very hands of God Himself, who knows us better than we even know ourselves.

Getting back to "What if ": if this is all true, what does this mean for us? A better way to live with someone who is already there, ready to help, and knows every day of our lives as though it has already happened—knew it before we were even a tiny spot in our mother's womb. Wow!

The book of Psalms is another great collection to read through. It is 150 chapters long. Some are short, and some are longer, with Psalm 119 containing the most verses in the entire Bible totaling 176! But as in Proverbs, there is wisdom, history, and life lessons for how to live contained in the book, so I pray you will take the time soon to read through it all. And, of course, keep "What if " in mind!

The Old Testament contains so much history and is the story that leads up to Christ's birth, which happens in the New Testament. When you are ready for a full read through of the Word, read it as a story. Much in the Old Testament is repetitive. You will read the same history a few times in parts of it, which add to what was written before. It can be a bit difficult, maybe even boring at times, but what we must remember this is God's inspired Word for us! The history matters, the wisdom given matters, and it can change our lives for the better. The history of the Israelites is often mirrored in our own lives, just in a different time and culture. In reading it, I get so frustrated with how stubborn they were and how quickly they walked away from the God who rescued them so many times—only to be convicted that I am the same way! My human nature causes me so often to react unlovingly and sinfully, and yet, my Lord is still there, waiting for me to turn back to Him, and He always picks up the pieces and sets me right again, just as He did for the Israelites.

The Old Testament contains the books of Ruth and Esther, stories of two women we can learn a lot from in how to live sacrificially and faithfully. Another book, Song of Songs, also called Song of Solomon, is a complete and total love story! The Old Testament ends with several books about prophets sent to the Israelites by God Himself telling them of their need to turn from their sin and back to Him. Also keep in mind that throughout this testament are predictions of One to come, a Savior, who would bring deliverance from sin!

As we turn our focus to the New Testament in the rest of this book (with occasional glances back at the Old Testament), I wanted you to have an understanding of what you can expect to find when you begin your read through of this historical, wisdom-filled story.

Chapter 4

First, I want to start off this chapter by saying there is so much more in the Bible that shows a beautiful way to live, and this book is nowhere close to being all-inclusive. My prayer here is to get us thinking about living a better life and getting some powerful tips on how to do that.

As we head into the New Testament, we need a little background. The Gospels—the first four books of the New Testament, Matthew, Mark, Luke, and John—give us a look at the life and ministry of Jesus from different perspectives, some with more detail and backstory, and all worth reading.

Let's take a moment to look at who Jesus is—God incarnate, who came to live fully as man and fully God for a time on our earth. He came to do a very special task which is to take the sins of His created people upon Himself, die as our final sacrifice for that sin, be resurrected, and overcome that barrier once and for all, so all who believe in Him shall spend eternity in His presence.

He was born as we are born. His mother was Mary, a virgin, who was betrothed to Joseph. We will read a bit of their story now. You know the drill. Get out that Bible, and go read Luke 1:26–38, then come back here for further discussion.

Hello and welcome back! Starting in verse 26, we see the angel Gabriel visiting Mary, explaining that she is blessed among women and will soon bring forth a Son. His name is to be Jesus. It also tells us that He, Jesus, would be the Son of the Highest. Even more fantastic is the fact that Mary will become pregnant by the Holy Spirit coming upon her, not in the traditional way experienced by the rest of humanity.

At first, as seen in verse 29, Mary was "troubled" at what Gabriel was saying to her. Trouble in this verse comes from the Greek word *diatarasso* meaning to disturb wholly, to agitate greatly, trouble greatly. I think we must take a moment to discuss why she would be greatly troubled.

First, she is a virgin, meaning she has never been with a man to become pregnant.

Second, in this culture, being pregnant outside of wedlock was grounds for disgrace and often your entire family disowning you!

Third, wouldn't you be a little scared, freaked out, and unsettled if an angel appeared and started saying these things to you?

But Gabriel tells Mary to not be afraid, that she has found "favor with God." Favor here comes from the word *charis*, meaning graciousness: that which affords joy, pleasure, delight, sweetness, loveliness. This tells us that Mary must have a great love for God, lived her life for Him, and had a relationship with Him.

Gabriel goes on to tell Mary that Jesus will be the fulfillment of Old Testament prophecy given to David in 2 Samuel 7:12–18.

Just a quick side note, the entire Bible is *all* about Jesus, and throughout the Old Testament we see many precursors and prophecies of Christ's coming. David's story is worth reading especially for the history that is given there. More is found about him in the Old Testament books of 1 and 2 Samuel, 1 and 2 Kings, and 1 Chronicles. He also authored many of the Psalms.

Mary does question Gabriel in verse 34 about how this can possibly come to fruition since she has never "known a man" referring to "sexually" in order to get pregnant, to which the angel answers her, "The Holy Spirit will come upon you!" This was so that Jesus would be called "the Son of God."

In verse 38, we see Mary conceding, showing such great faith by saying, "Let it be to me according to your word."

We must pause a moment to look for a "What if " here. What if Mary had just dismissed Gabriel? What if she had simply walked away and not had the heart to do as God was calling her? She would have missed out on the biggest blessing of her life—being the mother of the Savior of the world.

This brings me to another question: if Mary had said no, would Jesus have not been born then? My answer to that is I believe He still would have, just a different momma would have been used. But what we need to understand here is God knew the story, beginning to end already, and that back in the Old Testament and the stories told of Jesus coming, the family lines had already been laid in place. The genealogy had been given already, and Joseph's family history came from that genealogy. So even though Joseph wasn't biologically Christ's father, his part was just as important as Mary's. To fully understand this, you must go read through the Old Testament. Since I am writing this book as more of an introduction to the Bible, and hopefully sparking interest to go read it all the way through for yourself, we are barely scraping the surface of all there is to this part of the story.

At this time, we need to look at Jesus and why His birth was needed to begin with. Remember back to the first chapter of this book and the first book of the Bible, Genesis? That tells us why. Genesis 3 gives a thorough explanation of the temptation and fall of man with Eve biting that fruit and sharing with her husband Adam. That one act allowed evil to be released. It, unfortunately, gave Satan a chance to try (in his own mind) to do what he has always wanted to do, which was to be God himself. He has always had a bad side, and his whole mission is to separate us from God, our creator. That one act, the bite of the fruit, was, in his eyes, his first success because it took away full obedience to God. It created a chasm, a separation between man and God. It took Adam and Eve's eyes off God, creating a war humanity has faced ever since, the free will to choose between good and evil.

From that point forward, our sin has kept us from the ideal relationship God desired to have with us—one where He physically is always present with us—as He was with Adam and Eve in the garden before the bite of the fruit. He is holy; we are not. But Jesus' birth was the answer to that problem. He had to be born, so that He could become our Savior—our ultimate sacrifice for sin by His shed blood and death on the cross. I am still awed and amazed by my God, who seeks relationship with me to the point of taking my deserved punishment for sin, so I can spend eternity with Him. That is unconditional love for sure.

I want to pause a moment to go over the impact of sacrifice and why that was so important. Once again, let's refer back to Genesis 3:21 and note the first bloodshed for man and by whom it was shed:

> Also for Adam and his wife the Lord God
> made tunics of skin and clothed them.

Now, this is after they have sinned and taken a bite of the fruit. This is after they hid themselves from God because they were naked and afraid. Obviously, the "tunics of skin" had to come from animals that died, thus shedding of blood. And it was the *LORD*, *yhwh*, Himself who did this to clothe His beloved. That is huge to me. He still shows His love for them, and provides for them, even in their sin. He has done that for all of us again in Jesus' death on the cross—His own blood pouring from His head from the crown of thorns and from His pierced side. His pain and bloodshed covering *all* sin; the final blood sacrifice needed.

For a more in-depth look at sin offerings, read Leviticus 4. It gives you the "101" of sacrificing. I am very thankful that I do not have to do that for every sin—intentional and unintentional.

I think this leads to an important "What if" question. What if our *Lord* had not made this plan of salvation? Where would we be? We would still be sacrificing animals with no hope of eternal life with Him. For me this "what if" question is almost ludicrous because of what we have already seen in our little bit of reading the Bible and knowing the Lord knew the beginning and the end before it even existed. He had a plan for our salvation and eternal life—His Son Jesus Christ!

Chapter 5

It is time to look at what is commonly referred to as "the Trinity." An interesting thought here is that you will not find "the Trinity" written in the Bible anywhere. That is terminology used for the collective persons of Father, Son (Jesus), and Holy Spirit. Another good reason to read the Bible for yourself is we are told there is a lot in there that is not, or that it says certain things and means certain things but that is not always correct. The only way to know for yourself what it says is to read it.

The Bible speaks of three persons throughout the Bible in the Old and New Testament:

1. Father—seen in several forms such as God, Lord, LORD.
2. Son—Jesus Christ.
3. The Holy Spirit—often just seen as Spirit.

The Bible is full of verses that speak about these three persons and who they are. It will take some time to find and read them all, but I encourage you to do this, and I think you will be amazed at what you learn along the way.

For this chapter we start with a look at a passage from the Old Testament, book of Isaiah. Grab your Bible and go to Isaiah 48 and read verses 12–19. See you when you get back!

For those of you who may not know who Isaiah was, he was a prophet from God who was called to speak out about the sins of the culture at that time. This is my simple way of defining it. Isaiah spoke to three historical epochs, meaning distinctive periods in history, delivering messages of condemnation and judgment in chapters 1–39, comfort for exiles in 40–55, and encouraged the Jewish exiles who have returned to their land in the last chapters of the book.

That is just a side note for a little context. What we are interested in is the verses that speak specifically of these three persons. First, this is Jesus speaking the words we read in 12–19, and remember, this is the Old Testament. (As you read through the Bible you will soon see that all three persons are included throughout both testaments.) Verses 16–17 makes very clear that Jesus is speaking here:

> 16   Come near to Me (Jesus), hear this:
> I have not spoken in secret from the beginning;
> from the time that it was, I was there.
> And now the Lord God (Father) /and His Spirit
> have sent Me.
> 17   Thus says the Lord, your Redeemer, The
> Holy One of Israel:
> I am the Lord your God
> Who teaches you to profit,
> Who leads you by the way you should go.

Let's look at some of these words in the original language.

Lord, adonay, the Lord is a proper name of God only. Verse 16. (One of many names for God.)

God/LORD: *yhwh,* self-existent or eternal; name of God, the proper name of the one true God. God in verse 16 and LORD in verse 17. (Remember, all caps indicates the use of *yhwh* throughout the Bible.)

Spirit: *ruah,* wind, breath, mind. Verse 16 (When Spirit is capitalized it refers to the Holy Spirit.)

Redeemer: *ga'al,* to redeem, act as kinsman, redeemer, avenge, revenge, ransom. Verse 17

Holy One: *qados* or *qadosh,* sacred, God, holy, saint, set apart. Verse 17

God: *elohiym*, plural of gods in the ordinary sense, but when referring to God of the Bible it means of the Supreme God. Verse 17. (Another name for God).

There is a lot of great stuff just in these verses, but a deeper study will have to wait for another time. I hope you agree that just this one passage of scripture shows us clearly three persons—God/Father, Jesus/Son, Holy Spirit. It also shows something else about Jesus in verses 12–13:

> Listen to Me, O Jacob, and Israel,
> My called: I am He, I am the First,
> I am also the Last.
> Indeed My hand has laid the
> foundation of the earth,
> and My right hand has stretched
> out the heavens;
> when I call to them,
> they stand up together.

Remember who is talking here? Jesus! These verses are very clear that He is telling us He is one with God, the "I am" verses, He, First, Last. Also, the reference to His "right hand has laid the foundation of the earth and has stretched out the heavens."

Are you getting excited about the Word of God yet? I pray this sparks a desire in you to study the Word and see what other treasures you can find. We have only looked at one passage that touches on this subject of three persons, and there are at least a hundred more throughout the Bible.

Before we move on, I want us to read a New Testament passage that corresponds with what we just read in Isaiah. John 1:1-5 (NKJV):

> In the beginning was the Word, and the
> Word was with God, and the Word was God. He
> was in the beginning with God. All things were

made through Him, and without Him nothing was made that was made. In Him was life, and the life was the light of men. And the light shines in the darkness, and the darkness did not comprehend it.

Here again, we see direct reference to Christ (the Word) and who He is:

1. In the beginning
2. With God
3. The Word was God
4. All things were made through Him
5. Without Him nothing was made
6. In Him is the life and light of men
7. His light shines in the darkness
8. The darkness does not comprehend it

The Bible has so many more references to this, that a deeper study of this is needed. I pray you will take the time very soon to look for more on your own.

I do want to touch on the Holy Spirit a little more. It is important to see what role He plays for clarity. I highly recommend reading through the entire Gospel of John, but for the moment let's narrow our focus to John 15:26–27 and John 16:5–15. A quick background here: This is Jesus speaking. He is talking to His disciples about His pending death and the Helper (Holy Spirit) to come. Go read through these verses, and meet me back here.

Looking specifically at verses 13–15 we see who the Holy Spirit is:

1. He guides us into all truth.
2. He speaks what He hears from Christ.
3. He tells us things to come.
4. He glorifies Christ.

Verse 15 gives a look at the oneness of these three persons: "All things that the Father has are Mine. Therefore, I said He will take of Mine and declare it to you."

Below are a few more scriptures that look at the Holy Spirit. This is by no means an exhaustive list. My hope is you will embark on a study of your own soon and find more.

- The Spirit brings wisdom, understanding, counsel, knowledge and fear (awe of the Lord):

  The Spirit of the Lord shall rest upon Him, the Spirit of wisdom and understanding, the Spirit of counsel and might, the Spirit of knowledge and of the fear of the Lord. (Isaiah 11:2 NKJV)

- We receive power to witness from the Spirit:

  But you shall receive power when the Holy Spirit has come upon you; and you shall be witnesses to Me in Jerusalem, and in all Judea and Samaria, and to the end of the earth. (Acts 1:8 NKJV)

- The Spirit is our Helper and teaches us:

  But the Helper, the Holy Spirit, whom the Father will send in My name, He will teach you all things that I said to you. (John 14:26 NKJV)

- The Spirit helps in our weakness and prays on our behalf:

  Likewise, the Spirit also helps in our weaknesses. For we do not know what we should pray for as we ought, but the Spirit Himself makes intercession for us with groanings which cannot be uttered. Now He, who searches the hearts knows what the mind of the Spirit is, because He makes intercession for the saints according to the will of God. (Romans 8:26–27 NKJV)

What if? Can you find your own "What if" statements here? For me today, mine are the following: What if I deepen my reliance on the Holy Spirit, learn to listen to what He is telling me, which comes directly from the Father and Jesus? What if that would make me better equipped to help others in this world that is often so difficult to navigate?

There is so much to learn about the Holy Spirit and the power and wisdom we receive from Him, and I pray you will take the time for further study.

For me, I sum up "the Trinity" as this: three persons, one God; three roles, one God. Let's look at an egg as one example, a visual in a way. There is the yolk, the white, the shell, but one egg. All three separate parts, but still one!

Chapter 6

Before I began writing this book, I felt the Lord urging that one chapter must be set aside for a specific look at what are known as the sexual sins and the Biblical definition of marriage. I know this is a very touchy subject, especially in today's world. So, let's start off with a "What if" question first.

What if the world, and more specifically believers, followed the guidance of the Word in the areas of sex and marriage?

Keeping this question in mind, let's go see what the Bible says. We must first look back to Genesis again. It is important to remember that we were formed in the image of God, and He created us male and female as we read in chapter one from Genesis 1:27 and Genesis 2:18–25.

So two things we must understand here:

1. We are created in God's image.
2. We were created as male and female, man and woman.

These two statements are the foundation for biblical marriage, and ultimately the reason for the laws concerning sexual sin. Mark 10:6–9 (NKJV):

> But from the beginning of the creation,
> God made them male and female. For this reason
> a man shall leave his father and mother and be
> joined to his wife, and the two shall become one

flesh. Therefore, what God has joined together, let not man separate.

This, my friends, is the protocol for biblical marriage:

1. Male and female
2. Become one flesh
3. What God has joined together

We will look up some more scripture now, so pull out your Bible. And please keep in mind that there are many more verses to read through than I have posted here. Hopefully in the near future, you can take some time to search out more for yourself.

Please read Ephesians 5:22–33, then meet me back here for a breakdown.

Ready?

1. Wives submit to your husband as to the Lord. Verse 22
2. The husband is the head of the wife, as Christ is head of the church and Savior of the body. Verse 23–24
3. Husbands love your wives, as Christ loves the church and gave Himself for her. Verse 25–29
4. We are members of His body, His flesh, and His bones. Verse 30
5. Man shall leave his father and mother, be joined to his wife and the two shall become one flesh. Verse 31

Then in verse 32, we read why this is important:

This is a great mystery, but I speak concerning Christ and the church.

Biblical marriage is a reflection of Christ's love for His church. It is sacred. It is sacrificial. It is a commitment. It is unconditional love.

Looking at marriage leads to our next topic that is always contentious, especially in unbelievers, but to my surprise even with many believers—sexual sin. 1 Corinthians 6:18–20 (NKJV) tells us:

> Flee sexual immorality. Every sin that a man does is outside the body, but he who commits sexual immorality sins against his own body. Or do you not know that your body is the temple of the Holy Spirit who is in you, whom you have from God, and you are not your own? For you were bought at a price; therefore, glorify God in your body and in your spirit, which are God's.

Let's look at what sexual immorality means in the original language here. It is the Greek word *porneia*: harlotry. It is illicit sexual intercourse defined as adultery, fornication, homosexuality, lesbianism, intercourse with animals, incest.

I find it very interesting, in these verses, the fact that sexual immorality is sin against our own body. There is a difference between sexual sin and other sin. Why? Here it tells us it is because our body is the temple for the Holy Spirit who is in us and that our bodies are not our own. Remember who created us? Remember who died to save us from our sin? Jesus—in His sacrificial death for our sin on the cross.

I want to share here from my own personal experience that sexual sin affects us physically, mentally, emotionally, and deep down in our souls in ways we cannot comprehend. For me, it caused years of feeling I was a failure. I was not good enough to find "true love" and marriage. I didn't deserve my Savior's love and sacrifice for me. So many lies were used by the enemy (Satan) to keep me from living in connection with my Lord. I am happy to say I no longer feel this way because the Lord showed me His unconditional, sacrificial love. He led me to Psalm 139 and showed me who I really am—His creation! Let's back up a few verses in 1 Corinthians 6 and go read verses 9–20. Then we will meet back here and look at some definitions for words we find here.

Ready? Tough verses, big words, so let's define some of these now. Again, looking at the original language of Greek we will find the definitions for each word below.

Fornicators: *pornos* (similar sounding to *pornea* from earlier), a man who prostitutes his body to another's lust for hire; male prostitute; a man who indulges in unlawful sexual intercourse (premarital sex).

Idolaters: *eidololatres*, a worshipper of false gods;

Adulterers: *moichos*, sexual intercourse between a married person and a person who is not his or her spouse;

Homosexuals: *malakos*, soft, soft to the touch; effeminate; a boy kept for homosexual relations with a man; a male who submits his body to unnatural lewdness;

Sodomites: *arsenokoites*, one who lies with a male as with a female, sodomite, homosexual;

Thieves: *kleptes*. an embezzler, pilferer;

Covetous: *pleonektes*, one eager to have more, especially what belongs to others;

Drunkards: *methysos*, intoxicated, tipsy;

Revilers: *loidoros*, abusive, one who scoffs, insults, censures or reproaches;

Extortionist: *harplax*, rapacious, extortion, a robber.

As you can see this list contains more than sexual sins, but I thought you might like to see the Greek words and the definitions for each. I looked up each of these in my *Olive Tree Bible App* using the New King James Version of the Bible with Strong's Concordance attached.

There are many more verses on marriage and sexual sin in the Bible, contained in both testaments—Old and New. I pray that you will go and search them out especially if there is something that you have questions about.

Chapter 7

I feel a look at Hebrews 11 and some very faithful people whose stories are included in the Bible is a good way to draw this book to a close.

First, an explanation of what faith is in Hebrews 11:1–3 (NKJV):

> Now faith is the substance of things hoped for, the evidence of things not seen. For by it the elders obtained a good testimony. By faith we understand that the worlds were framed by the word of God, so that the things which are seen were not made of things which are visible.

Essentially, faith is belief in someone we don't see with our eyes physically but we do know is real. We know deep inside. We can "see" with our spirit. We can see the evidence of Him all around us through His creation. Take a flower, for example. See the detail in the stem, leaves, and petals, the beautiful array of colors. That is God's creation!

He also gave us people to look at and see how they lived by faith as great examples. We will look at several "Hall of Fame" people now. We will meet sinners, like ourselves, but people who stayed the course in their faith in God. Grab your Bible now and go read Hebrews 11. This chapter is a beautiful (although not inclusive) summary of God's people and stories contained within His story—His Word. I will be waiting right here for you.

Well? What do you think of that? I still get chills reading this chapter. Let's summarize what we saw here.

By faith:

Abel offered to God a more excellent sacrifice than Cain. (Genesis 4:3–15)

Enoch was taken away so that he did not see death because he pleased God. (Genesis 5:21–24)

Noah, moved with godly fear, prepared the ark for saving his household. (Genesis 6:13–22)

Abraham obeyed when he was called to leave his home to receive his promised inheritance. (Genesis 12:1–4)

Sarah bore a child in her old age. (Genesis 18:11–14)

Abraham was willing to offer his only son, Isaac, back to the Lord. (Genesis 22:1–14)

Isaac blessed Jacob and Esau. (Genesis 27:26–40)

Jacob blessed each of the sons of Joseph. (Genesis 48:1, 5, 16, 20)

Joseph made mention of the departure of the children of Israel and gave instructions for his bones. (Genesis 50:24; Exodus 13:19) (For Joseph's whole story, see Genesis 30–50.)

Moses was hidden as a baby by his family to save his life. (Exodus 2:1–3)

Moses refused to be called Pharaoh's son, choosing to go back to his own people. (Exodus 2:11–15)

Moses forsook Egypt, kept the Passover, passed through the Red Sea, and led the people of Israel out of captivity and slavery. (Book of Exodus contains this historical story.)

The walls of Jericho fell. (Joshua 6:20)

Rahab did not perish after helping the spies. (Joshua 2:1–21; 6:17–25)

Others mentioned:

Gideon (Judges 6:11; 7:1–25)

Barak (Judges 4:6–24)

Samson (Judges 13:24–16:31)

Jephthah (Judges 11:1–29; 12:1–7)

David (1 Samuel 16:17. For all of David's story read through 1 and 2 Samuel, 1 and 2 Kings. He also wrote many of the Psalms.)

Samuel (1 Samuel 7:9–14. Read 1 Samuel for the whole story.)

The above names were attributed for subduing kingdoms, working righteousness, obtaining promises, stopping the mouths of lions, quenching the violence of fire, escaping the sword, in weakness made strong, valiant in battle, turning to fight the armies of enemies, raising the dead, being tortured, imprisoned, stoned, sawn in two, tempted, slain with the sword, wandering in destitution, afflicted, tormented, had to hide for safety. And the chapter ends with these two verses that speak volumes to us:

> And all these, having obtained a good testimony through faith, did not receive the promise, God having provided something better for us, that they should not be made perfect apart from us. (Hebrews 11:39–40 NKJV)

Telling us that these imperfect people, just like us: sinful, broken, hurting people, were all still used by God even in their imperfection. Their faith allowed them to proceed forward even when they could not see what the outcome would be, and some never saw the final work of their faith.

What if we could live our lives with faith like this? Seeking His direction, following it in the power of the Holy Spirit, and our desire to serve Him, and make life better for those around us, and yes, even for ourselves! A life free of condemnation and spite, just loving all as He calls us to, and allowing Him to do the work as He is the only one equipped to do it anyway.

In closing, let's review some "What if" questions:

What if, as the Word tells us, God, Jesus, and the Holy Spirit are one?

What if He had a plan to save us from the sins we are guilty of committing?

Matthew 15:19 (NKJV) tells us,

> For out of the heart come evil thoughts, murders, adulteries, fornications, thefts, false witness, slanders.

What if He—as our God, our Creator, knowing that we were going to sin and fall short of being worthy to stand in His presence—made a plan to take the punishment we deserved?

A closer look at the Gospel accounts shows us what Jesus did. He came to save the lost, heal the sick, and love all. And then He was taken and imprisoned, found guilty, and punished to death on a cross after being scourged, beaten, tortured—all for crimes He did not commit. Why? To fulfill a promise He made to us. A provision of final sacrifice, a shedding of blood to cover the sin we committed, wipe it away, completely gone forever, making it possible for us to stand with Him once again; holy and blameless, worthy to be in His presence.

What if God has given us a helper, the Holy Spirit, to walk with us?

In John 14:16 and 26, Jesus promises us that the Father will send an advocate who will teach us all things, bring to remembrance the scripture, give us wisdom, someone who is with us forever! We have a very real helpmate to help us navigate this thing called life. Wow! What if?

What if we read the Bible, His inspired Word, and live by it, loving Him, loving our neighbors?

There are many more "What if" statements we could take and use from the Bible. I plan to continue my research and watch for them, and then apply them to my life, and encourage others to do the same. What if all humanity would take up this way of living? What changes would we see? Life here could be a glimpse of what heaven has in store for us.

What if?

NKJV Study Bible
Third Edition
Thomas Nelson, 2018
Olive Tree Bible Software, 1998–2022

About the Author

Loni Hunley grew up in the quaint town of Bishop, California. She loves reading, spending time with family, and studying God's Word. Her debut book, What If? is a direct result of stepping outside her comfort zone and obeying the Lord's whisper to encourage others to read His word for themselves.

www.ingramcontent.com/pod-product-compliance
Lightning Source LLC
Chambersburg PA
CBHW051251120626
46547CB00014B/1895